P9-DFF-274

Hey there, grown-ups!

Thank you for buying *The Do It Myself Kids' Cookbook* for the shorter chefs in your life. Before you turn the show over to any young foodies, you should read the following words of wisdom regarding kitchen safety and set-up, as well as suggestions for how best to use this book.

THE Do It Myself KIDS' COOKBOOK

NOTHING SHARP, NOTHING HOT!

BY LAURIE GOLDRICH WOLF

PHOTOGRAPHS BY BRUCE WOLF · ILLUSTRATIONS BY MATT SHAY

downtown bookworks

CONTENTS

To begin...

ALL SMALL CHEFS MUST:

- Wash hands with soap and warm water before they set foot in the kitchen. And none of this lick-and-a-promise stuff— get a nice lather of soap going, then rinse, and dry.

- Tie back long hair.

- Listen to the grown-ups in charge.

ALL GROWN-UPS IN CHARGE SHOULD:

- Clear a workspace with chairs that are at a comfortable height for the chefs.

- Keep a roll of kraft/butcher paper on hand to cover the workspace. Tape it down with masking tape; it makes clean-up a breeze.

- Provide aprons and a stack of clean kitchen towels for chefs to wipe their hands on periodically.

- Wash all fresh fruits and vegetables thoroughly before putting them out in the measured quantities indicated in the recipes.

- Pay attention to the expiration dates on food items that carry them. They are there for a reason. For that matter, smell stuff. If you think it smells funny, throw it out. Better safe than sick.

- Look lively. DO NOT assume you can stop paying attention once the workspace, tools, and ingredients have been set up. Children this age still require close supervision around any activity—including the ones in this book.

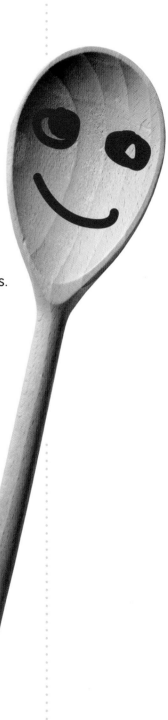

A WORD OR TWO ABOUT THE RECIPES AND CHOOSING WHAT TO MAKE:

- Become familiar with the tools and ingredients lists in the book. You will see a definite pattern of repeated tools (lots of plastic knives, cutting boards, big bowls, wooden spoons, etc.) and kid-friendly foods (lots of berries, cheese, cold cuts, crackers, pasta, and cookies). Most of the ingredients are staples in the pantry/refrigerator of any home in which a school-age kid resides.

- At the back of the book you will find an ingredients index. If you have sliced turkey you'd like to use up, strawberries that would be most delicious eaten TODAY, or a child who can't ever eat enough corn, this ingredients index will be the most efficient way to approach the question, "What shall we make?"

- Save recipes that call for anything as "ambitious" as pre-cooked chicken breasts or fried chicken breasts for days when you have them as leftovers, rather than broiling or frying up a batch on the spot. These recipes were designed for turning leftovers into a yummy dish. Also, we've provided basic recipes for dressings, but if you have others you prefer, feel free to use them.

- The extent of the grown-up preparation in the book is minimal; really not much more than cooking (or pulling out leftover) pasta, hard-boiling eggs, coring and slicing apples, or toasting bread. When putting out liquid ingredients such as milk or water, you can decide whether a milk carton or a pitcher of water goes on the workspace with an empty measuring cup or whether you will be pre-measuring.

- To vastly cut down on grown-up prep, ingredients such as shredded carrots and shredded cheese may be purchased in their lovely bagged form. Of course, the correct amount can always be hand-shredded by the grown-up in charge. Kitchen shredders and/or graters aren't the most kid-friendly utensils. Shaved knuckle, not so fun.

- Most of the recipes serve 1 or 2 kids. If they serve more, we've let you know.

LIST OF PANTRY ITEMS TO HAVE ON HAND

STAPLES: almond butter, bagels, bread, chocolate chips, Chex® cereal, chocolate frosting, chopped dates, cookies, crisped rice cereal, dried apricots, dried cranberries, golden raisins, graham crackers, granola, honey, Honey Nut Cheerios®, ice cream cones, marshmallow creme, pasta, peanut butter, pita, rice, Ritz® crackers, salsa, shredded coconut, small pretzels, sprinkles, strawberry and chocolate syrups, sugar, tortillas, vanilla instant pudding mix, vanilla wafers

CANNED GOODS: black beans, black olives, corn, crushed pineapple, garbanzo beans (chick peas), light red kidney beans, peas, roasted peppers, tuna

SPICES AND SEASONINGS: Dry mustard, garlic powder, olive oil, paprika, pepper, red wine vinegar, salt, sesame oil, soy sauce, Worcestershire sauce

FRESH FRUITS AND VEGETABLES: apples, avocados, bananas, blueberries, cherry tomatoes, cucumbers, lettuce, peaches, pears, raspberries, fresh peppers, seedless grapes, shredded carrots, strawberries, tomatoes

LIST OF FRIDGE ITEMS TO HAVE ON HAND

STAPLES: blue cheese, buttermilk, Cheddar cheese, cold cuts, cream cheese, Dijon mustard, hard-boiled eggs, hummus, ice cream, ketchup, lemon juice, mayonnaise, milk, mozzarella cheese, Muenster cheese, orange juice, Parmesan cheese, pesto, pickle relish, pickles, pink lemonade, plain and flavored yogurts, pound cake, salad dressings, seltzer, sour cream, strawberry jam, Swiss cheese, whipped cream, white grape juice, yellow mustard

Peanut Butter, Banana, Strawberry, and Coconut on Cinnamon Bread

TOOLS

- **Cutting board** ⋯⋯⋯⋯
- **Measuring spoons** ⋯⋯⋯⋯
- **Spreader** ⋯⋯⋯⋯
- **Plastic knife** ⋯⋯⋯⋯

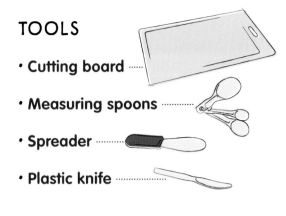

INGREDIENTS

- **3 slices cinnamon raisin bread** ⋯⋯⋯⋯
- **2 tablespoons peanut butter** ⋯⋯
- **1 small banana** ⋯⋯⋯⋯
- **1 tablespoon honey** ⋯⋯⋯⋯
- **3–4 strawberries** ⋯⋯⋯⋯
- **2 tablespoons coconut** ⋯⋯⋯⋯

GROWN-UP PREP: none

1. On a cutting board, plop 2 tablespoons of peanut butter on a slice of bread. Using a spreader, smooth the peanut butter to the edges of the bread.

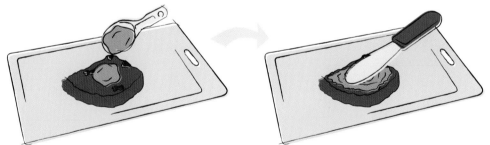

2. Peel the banana. On the cutting board, use a plastic knife to slice the banana into thin slices. Place the banana slices on the peanut butter—they'll stick nicely.

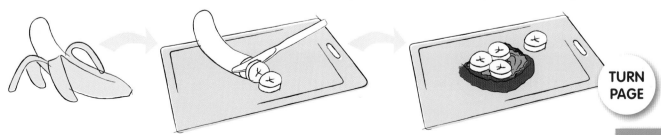

TURN PAGE

3. Place the next slice of bread on top of the banana slices. Squeeze or measure 1 tablespoon of honey. Drizzle the honey over the top slice of bread. Use the spreader to cover the whole slice of bread with the honey.

4. On the cutting board, use a plastic knife to slice the strawberries into thin slices. Lay the strawberry slices on top of the honey.

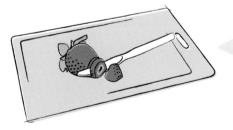
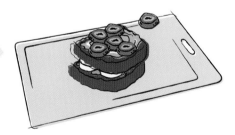

5. Sprinkle 2 tablespoons of coconut over the strawberry slices.

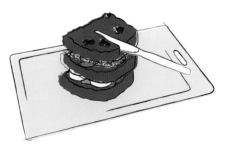

6. Place the last slice of bread on top of the strawberries and coconut. Gently cut with the plastic knife, or eat without cutting. This sandwich can be a little messy, but it tastes so good, who cares!

Hard-boiled Egg, Apple, and Chicken Salad on Crisps

TOOLS

- **Cutting board**
- **Plastic knife**
- **Small Plate**
- **Fork**
- **Measuring spoons**
- **Bowl**
- **Wooden spoon**

INGREDIENTS

- **1 hard-boiled egg**
- **1 cooked chicken breast**
- **2 tablespoons mayonnaise**
- **1 teaspoon mustard**
- **1 tablespoon shredded carrots**
- **1 scallion**
- **Salt**
- **3 Finn crisps®**
- **2 apple quarters**

GROWN-UP PREP: 1 hard-boiled egg, peeled; 1 cooked chicken breast; 1 apple, cored and quartered

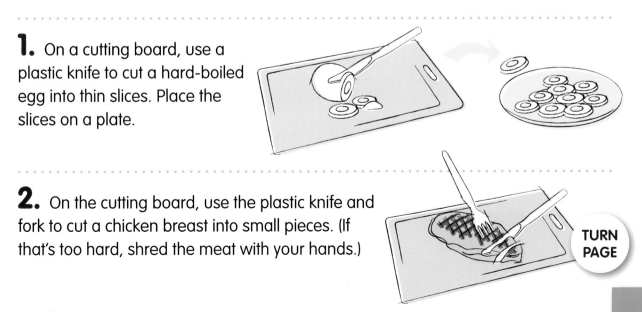

1. On a cutting board, use a plastic knife to cut a hard-boiled egg into thin slices. Place the slices on a plate.

2. On the cutting board, use the plastic knife and fork to cut a chicken breast into small pieces. (If that's too hard, shred the meat with your hands.)

TURN PAGE

3. Plop 2 tablespoons of mayonnaise and 1 teaspoon of mustard into a bowl. Using a wooden spoon, stir them together. Mix in 1 tablespoon of shredded carrots.

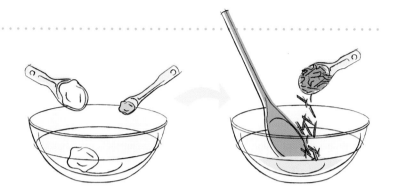

4. On the cutting board, use the plastic knife to slice a scallion very thinly. Mix the scallion slices in the bowl with the mayonnaise, mustard, and carrots.

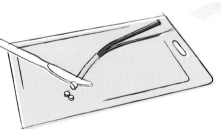

5. Add the chicken and a pinch of salt, and mix again.

6. Place the first Finn® crisp on the cutting board. Lay the egg slices on the crisp. Push it to the side.

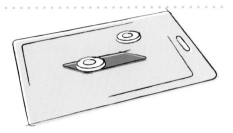

7. On the cutting board, use the plastic knife to cut 2 apple quarters into 3 thin slices. Lay the apple slices on top of the egg slices. Place a second crisp on top of the apple slices.

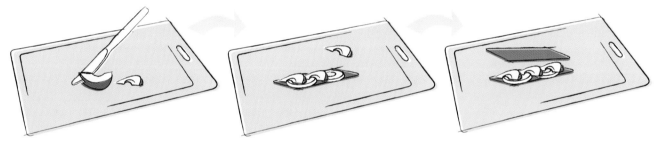

8. Using the wooden spoon, gently spread the chicken salad to the edges of the crisp. Top with the last Finn® crisp.

Cream Cheese, Strawberry, and Pineapple Quesadilla

TOOLS

• **Cutting board** ....

• **Measuring spoons** ....

• **Plastic knife** ....

INGREDIENTS

• 3 6-inch flour tortillas ....

• 2 tablespoons cream cheese at room temperature ....

• 5 tablespoons crushed pineapple ....

• 2 tablespoons strawberry jam ....

• 4 medium strawberries ....

GROWN-UP PREP: 1 can crushed pineapple, opened and drained into a bowl

1. On a cutting board, plop 2 tablespoons of cream cheese on 1 tortilla. Using a plastic knife, spread the cream cheese evenly over the tortilla.

TURN
PAGE

2. Plop 5 tablespoons of crushed pineapple on top of cream cheese. Use the plastic knife to spread the pineapple to the edges of the tortilla.

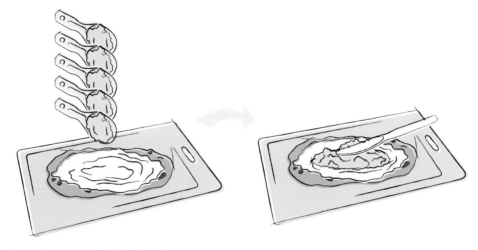

3. Place the second tortilla over the crushed pineapple. Plop 2 tablespoons of strawberry jam on the second tortilla. Using the plastic knife, spread the jam to the edges of the tortilla.

4. On the cutting board, use the plastic knife to thinly slice the strawberries. Place them on top of the jam.

5. Cover with the third tortilla. Using the plastic knife, cut the quesadilla into wedges.

 **SANDWICHES**

Honey, Berries, and Almond Butter on Graham Crackers

TOOLS

- **Cutting board**
- **Measuring spoons**
- **Butter knife**

INGREDIENTS

- 2 double graham crackers
- 2 tablespoons almond butter
- 12 raspberries
- 2 teaspoons honey

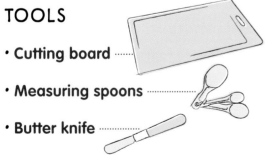

GROWN-UP PREP: nuttin' much

1. Over a cutting board, break 1 double graham cracker in half along the scored line.
Now, you have 2 square crackers.

2. Plop 1 tablespoon of almond butter on each graham cracker square. Using a butter knife, spread the almond butter to the edges.

3. Place the raspberries on top of the almond butter on each cracker (about 6 per cracker).

4. Squeeze or measure out 1 teaspoon of honey. Drizzle over the raspberries on a cracker. Repeat for other cracker.

5. Break the remaining graham cracker in half along the scored line to make 2 square crackers. Place 2 square crackers on top of the raspberries and honey. Enjoy!

Egg Salad with Red and Yellow Peppers on Flower Toast

TOOLS

- **Medium bowl**
- **Potato masher**
- **Measuring spoons**
- **Wooden spoon**
- **Cutting board**
- **Plastic knife**
- **Flower-shaped cookie cutter**

INGREDIENTS

- 2 hard-boiled eggs
- 3 tablespoons mayonnaise
- 1/4 teaspoon salt
- Black pepper
- 1/2 red pepper
- 1/2 yellow pepper
- 2 slices white bread, toasted

GROWN-UP PREP: 2 hard-boiled eggs, peeled; 2 slices white bread, toasted

24

1. Put 2 hard-boiled eggs in a bowl on your work surface. Using a potato masher, press down hard on the eggs, mashing them in the bowl until all the eggs are evenly squooshed.

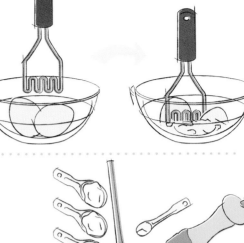

2. Plop 3 tablespoons of mayonnaise onto the mashed eggs. Add 1/4 teaspoon of salt and a few grinds of black pepper. Using a wooden spoon, stir everything together.

3. On a cutting board, use a plastic knife to cut the red and yellow peppers into the skinniest strips you can. They don't all have to be the same size. Push to the side of the cutting board.

4. Press a cookie cutter onto a piece of toast to make a flower-shaped piece of toast. Repeat on the second piece of toast.

5. Plop half the egg salad onto each piece of toast. Using the plastic knife, spread the egg salad evenly to the edges of the toast. Lay the skinny pieces of the red and yellow peppers on top of the egg salad.

Ham, Hard-boiled Egg, and Olives on Whole Wheat

TOOLS

- Cutting board
- Measuring spoons
- Butter knife
- Plastic knife

INGREDIENTS

- 1 slice whole wheat bread
- 1 teaspoon mayonnaise
- 2 slices baked or boiled ham
- 1 hard-boiled egg
- 4 pitted black olives

MAYONNAISE

BLACK OLIVES

GROWN-UP PREP: 1 hard-boiled egg, peeled; 1 can pitted black olives, opened, drained, and placed in a small bowl

1. On a cutting board, plop 1 teaspoon of mayonnaise on a slice of whole wheat bread. Using a butter knife, spread the mayonnaise to the edges of the bread.

2. Place 2 slices of ham on top of the bread.

3. On a cutting board, use a plastic knife to cut the egg into thin slices. Place the egg slices on top of the ham.

4. On the cutting board, use the plastic knife to cut the olives into thin slices. Place the olive slices on top of the hard-boiled egg slices. Cut the sandwich in quarters with a plastic knife or eat it whole.

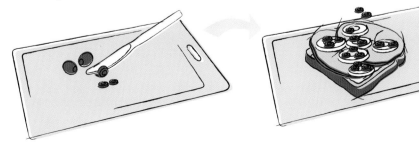

Turkey, Cheese, and Roasted Pepper Roll-ups

TOOLS

- **Cutting board**
- **Plastic knife**
- **Paper towels**
- **Toothpicks**

GROWN-UP PREP: relax

INGREDIENTS

- 1 6-inch flour tortilla
- 2 slices roast turkey
- 2 slices Cheddar cheese
- 1 whole roasted pepper from a jar

1. On a cutting board, place 2 slices of turkey on a tortilla, covering up as much tortilla as possible.

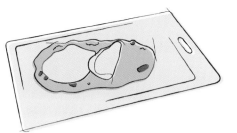

2. Place 2 slices of Cheddar cheese on the turkey. Push to the side.

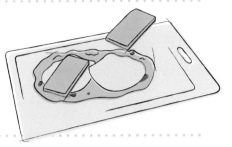

3. Place the roasted pepper on a paper towel and drain off any oil or liquid. On the cutting board, use a plastic knife to thinly slice the roasted pepper. Lay the pepper slices on top of the Cheddar cheese.

4. Roll up the tortilla, gently pressing it together as you roll so it will stick closed.

5. Using the plastic knife, slice the roll into 1-inch pieces. Push a toothpick into each roll to keep closed.

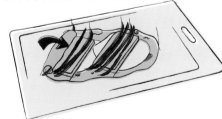

Shrimp Tacos with Avocado and Corn

TOOLS

- Cutting board
- Plastic knife
- Medium bowl
- Measuring spoons
- Wooden spoon

INGREDIENTS

- 6 small cooked shrimp
- 3 tablespoons canned or cooked corn
- 1/2 avocado
- 1 teaspoon lemon juice
- 2 tablespoons yogurt salsa (see page 70)
- 2 hard corn taco shells

GROWN-UP PREP: avocado, pitted and peeled; canned corn, opened and drained into a small bowl, or fresh corn, cut off the cob into a small bowl

1. On a cutting board, use a plastic knife to cut 6 shrimp into small pieces.

2. Put the shrimp in a bowl. Add 3 tablespoons of corn. Using a wooden spoon, mix the shrimp and corn.

3. On the cutting board, use a plastic knife to cut the avocado into small pieces. Add the avocado and 1 teaspoon of lemon juice to the bowl. Stir gently.

4. Add 2 tablespoons of yogurt salsa to the shrimp, corn, and avocado mixture. Gently stir the ingredients together.

5. Spoon the shrimp mixture into the taco shells.

Cheddar and Turkey with Mayo on Ritz® Crackers

TOOLS

- Cutting board
- Butter knife
- Measuring spoons
- Plastic knife

GROWN-UP PREP: nothing

INGREDIENTS

- 4 Ritz® crackers
- 2 slices Cheddar cheese
- 2 slices turkey
- 2 teaspoons mayonnaise
- 1 small cucumber, washed

1. On a cutting board, lay down 2 Ritz® crackers. Place 1 slice of Cheddar cheese on each cracker (the square cuts of Cheddar make the perfect cracker-size slices). Top each piece of Cheddar with 1 folded slice of turkey. (The slices may be bigger than the crackers, so fold the turkey until it is small enough to fit on the cracker, then place on top of the Cheddar.)

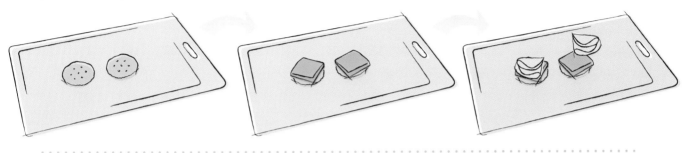

2. Using a butter knife, spread 1 teaspoon of mayonnaise on one side of the 2 remaining crackers. Push to the side.

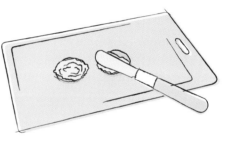

3. On the cutting board, use a plastic knife to cut 6 thin cucumber slices. Pile 3 thin slices of cucumber on each turkey-covered cracker.

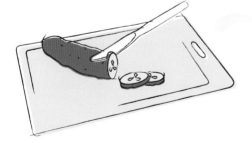

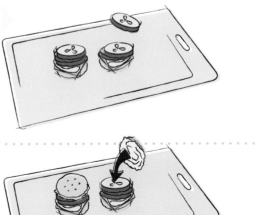

4. Top each cracker sandwich with the mayonnaise-covered crackers.

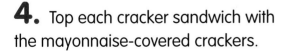

Cheddar, Ham, and Raisins on Whole Wheat Hearts

TOOLS

- Cutting board
- Measuring spoons
- 3- or 4-inch heart-shaped cookie cutter

INGREDIENTS

- 4 slices whole wheat bread
- 2 slices Cheddar cheese
- 2 slices baked ham
- 2 tablespoons Thousand Island dressing (see page 64)
- 2 tablespoons golden raisins

GROWN-UP PREP: absolutely zero

1. On a cutting board, slap 1 slice of Cheddar cheese each on 2 slices of whole wheat bread.

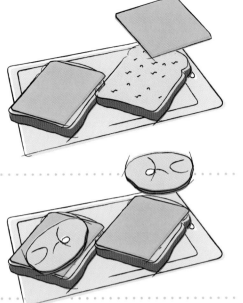

2. Top each piece of cheese with a slice of ham.

3. Spread each slice of ham with 1 tablespoon of Thousand Island dressing. Sprinkle 1 tablespoon of golden raisins on top of each sandwich.

4. Place the remaining 2 bread slices on top of the raisins to make 2 finished sandwiches. Using a cookie cutter, press down onto the first sandwich, pushing it all the way through the sandwich to cut out the shape. Gently remove the cookie cutter and repeat with the second sandwich.

Chicken, Peppers, and Shredded Cheddar Cheese in Lettuce Leaf Roll

TOOLS

- Cutting board
- Plastic knife
- Fork
- Measuring spoons

INGREDIENTS

- 1 cooked chicken breast
- 1/2 red pepper
- 2 large lettuce leaves
- 2 tablespoons shredded Cheddar cheese

GROWN-UP PREP: 1 cooked chicken breast

1. On a cutting board, use a plastic knife and fork to cut the cooked chicken breast into thin strips (or tear apart using your hands). Set aside.

2. On the cutting board, use the plastic knife to cut the red pepper into thin strips. Set aside.

3. On the cutting board, lay out the 2 lettuce leaves. Place even amounts of the chicken in the middle of each leaf. Place even amounts of the red pepper strips on top of the chicken, laying them down in the same direction as the chicken.

4. Sprinkle each of the lettuce leaves with 1 tablespoon of the shredded Cheddar cheese.

5. The lettuce will be your bread in this yummy sandwich. When you're ready to eat, roll or fold the lettuce around the chicken and veggies.

Cucumber, Carrot, and Hummus in a Pita

TOOLS

- **Cutting board**
- **Plastic knife**
- **Measuring spoons**

INGREDIENTS

- 1 pita bread
- 1 small cucumber
- 2 lettuce leaves
- 4 tablespoons shredded carrot
- 6 tablespoons hummus

GROWN-UP PREP: nothing

1. On a cutting board, use a plastic knife to cut the pita bread in half to make 2 half circles. Gently pry open each pita half, trying not to tear the bread, so that you end up with 2 bread "pockets."

2. On the cutting board, use the plastic knife to thinly slice the cucumber. Place 3 slices of cucumber in each pita pocket. Place a lettuce leaf in each pocket.

3. Place 2 tablespoons of shredded carrot into each pita pocket.

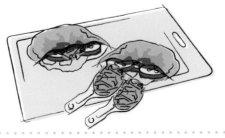

4. Spoon 3 tablespoons of hummus into each pita pocket.

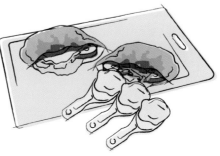

Tuna with Relish and Shredded Carrot in Mini Pitas

TOOLS

- **Small bowl**
- **Measuring spoons**
- **Fork**
- **Cutting board**
- **Plastic knife**

INGREDIENTS

- 1 small can tuna
- 2 tablespoons mayonnaise
- 1 tablespoon pickle relish
- 3 mini pita breads
- 1 tablespoon shredded carrot

GROWN-UP PREP: 1 can of tuna, opened, drained, and placed in a small bowl

1. Place a bowl of tuna securely on your work surface. Plop 2 tablespoons of mayonnaise into the bowl and mush with a fork until it is evenly mixed.

2. Add 1 tablespoon of relish and mush with the fork again.

3. On a cutting board, use a plastic knife to carefully slice each of the 3 mini pitas in half so that you end up with 6 small circles.

4. Plop 2 teaspoons of mixed tuna on each of the 3 pita bottoms and spread around to the edges.

5. Sprinkle 1 teaspoon of shredded carrot on top of the tuna on each sandwich. Top with the other halves of the pitas.

Roast Beef and Muenster with Mayo and Pickles on Mini Bagels

TOOLS

- Cutting board
- Plastic knife
- Measuring spoons

INGREDIENTS

- 2 slices roast beef
- 2 mini bagels
- 2 slices Muenster cheese
- 1 small pickle
- 2 teaspoons mayonnaise

GROWN-UP PREP: bagels, pre-cut

1. On a cutting board, place 1 slice of roast beef on each bagel bottom, folding to fit the bagel shape.

2. Top each piece of the roast beef with 1 Muenster cheese slice, folding again to fit.

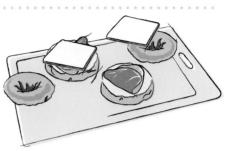

3. On the cutting board, use plastic knife to cut 6 thin pickle slices. Place 3 pickle slices on top of the cheese on each bagel.

4. Plop 1 teaspoon of mayonnaise on each bagel top. Use the plastic knife to spread the mayonnaise to the edge of each bagel. Place the bagel tops on top of the mayonnaise.

Roast Beef, Swiss, and Pickles in Lettuce Leaf Roll

TOOLS

- **Cutting board**
- **Plastic knife**
- **Measuring spoons**
- **Toothpicks**

INGREDIENTS

- 1 sour pickle
- 1 big piece romaine lettuce
- 1 tablespoon Thousand Island dressing (see page 64)
- 1 slice roast beef
- 1 slice Swiss cheese

GROWN-UP PREP: nada en particular

1. On a cutting board, use a plastic knife to cut the pickle in half the long way. Now you have 2 pieces of pickle. Cut each piece of pickle 1 more time the long way so you have 4 long pieces.

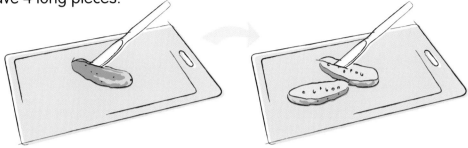

2. On the cutting board, lay out the lettuce leaf. Using the plastic knife, spread 1 tablespoon of Thousand Island dressing on the lettuce leaf.

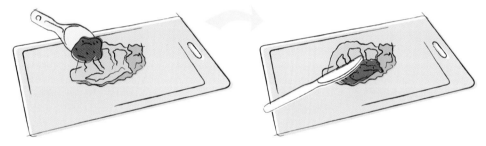

3. Pile the pickle slices in the middle of the lettuce leaf. Place the slice of roast beef on top of the pickle slices. Cover the roast beef with the slice of Swiss cheese.

4. Roll the lettuce around the meat and cheese. If you like, keep roll closed with a fun toothpick.

Turkey with Cranberry Sauce and Pear on a Bagel

TOOLS

- **Cutting board**
- **Measuring spoons**
- **Butter knife**
- **Plastic knife**

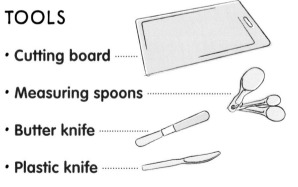

INGREDIENTS

- 1 cinnamon swirl bagel
- 3 tablespoons cranberry sauce
- 2 slices turkey
- 1 ripe pear

GROWN-UP PREP: 1 can of cranberry sauce, opened and placed in a small bowl; pear, washed and cored; bagel, pre-cut

1. On a cutting board, plop 2 tablespoons of cranberry sauce on the bottom slice of a bagel and use a butter knife to cover the bagel bottom with cranberry sauce. Spread the top slice with the other tablespoon of cranberry sauce.

2. Place 2 turkey slices on top of the cranberry sauce on the bagel bottom.

3. On the cutting board, use a plastic knife to thinly slice the cored pear. Lay 3 or 4 slices of pear on top of the turkey slices.

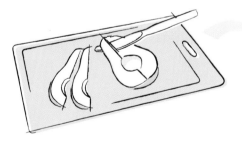 

4. Place the bagel top on the pear slices, and you're done.

Apple and Peanut Butter Puzzle

TOOLS

- **Cutting board**
- **Measuring spoons**
- **Butter knife**
- **Small plate**

INGREDIENTS

- **1 large apple**
- **4 tablespoons peanut butter**
- **2 teaspoons lemon juice**

GROWN-UP PREP: apple, cored and horizontally sliced; brush slices with lemon juice to prevent yucky browning

1. For this recipe you will rebuild the apple using peanut butter between the slices to hold them together. First, find the slice that was the very bottom of the apple and place it on a cutting board with the cut side up. Plop 1/2 tablespoon of peanut butter onto the slice and use a butter knife to spread it to the edges.

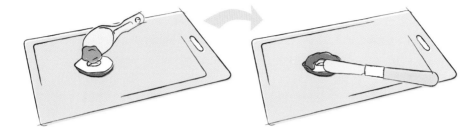

2. Find the next slice up from the bottom. Place it on top of the peanut butter and then spread about 1 tablespoon of peanut butter to the edges of that slice.

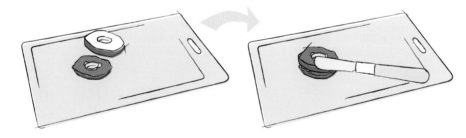

3. Continue rebuilding the apple, slice by slice, spreading each slice with the peanut butter, until you place the top of the apple in its original place. Put it on a plate. Eat your apple in reverse!

Dried Fruit Snack Mix or Cereal

TOOLS

- **Bowl, container, or Ziploc® bag**
- **Measuring cup**
- **Measuring spoons**
- **Wooden spoon**

INGREDIENTS

- 1 cup Chex® cereal
- 1 cup crisped rice cereal
- 1 cup graham cracker cereal
- 1 cup small pretzels
- 1 cup Honey Nut Cheerios®
- 6 tablespoons chocolate chips
- 6 tablespoons dried cranberries
- 6 tablespoons golden raisins
- 6 tablespoons chopped dates

GROWN-UP PREP: nada

Place a bowl, container, or bag securely on your work surface. All you need to do to make this tasty mix is combine all the ingredients in the bowl and gently stir it all up. It's great plain, with yogurt, or on top of ice cream.

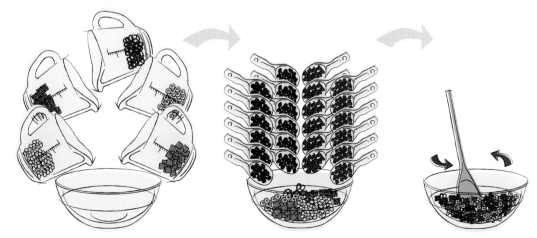

Granola Parfait

TOOLS

- **Cutting board**
- **Plastic knife**
- **Measuring spoons**
- **Parfait or sundae glass**

INGREDIENTS

- 2 strawberries
- 1 small container yogurt, any flavor
- 3 tablespoons granola

GROWN-UP PREP: relax and read the morning paper

1. On a cutting board, use a plastic knife to thinly slice the strawberries.

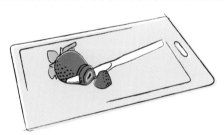

2. Plop 3 tablespoons of yogurt into a parfait glass.

TURN PAGE

3. Top with 1 tablespoon of granola.

4. Top the granola with several slices of strawberries and you've finished 1 parfait layer.

5. Repeat steps 2 through 4: 3 tablespoons yogurt + 1 tablespoon granola + a few strawberry slices. Repeat steps 2 through 4 a second time to fill the glass:

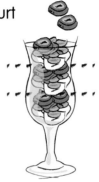

Dipped Fruit Slices with Peanut Butter and Cereal, Nuts, Chips, or Sprinkles

TOOLS

- 2 small bowls
- Measuring spoons
- 4 small plates or a plate with sections
- Cutting board
- Plastic knife
- Butter knife

INGREDIENTS

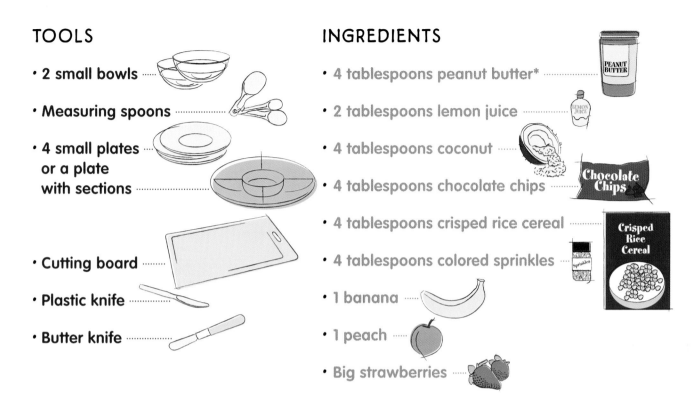

- 4 tablespoons peanut butter*
- 2 tablespoons lemon juice
- 4 tablespoons coconut
- 4 tablespoons chocolate chips
- 4 tablespoons crisped rice cereal
- 4 tablespoons colored sprinkles
- 1 banana
- 1 peach
- Big strawberries

GROWN-UP PREP: nuttin', honey
*For an especially sweet treat, substitute Nutella® chocolate hazelnut spread for peanut butter.

1. Place 2 small bowls on your work surface. Plop 4 tablespoons of peanut butter into one bowl. Measure 2 tablespoons of lemon juice into the other bowl.

TURN PAGE

continued Dipped Fruit Slices with Peanut Butter and Cereal, Nuts, Chips, or Sprinkles

2. Put 4 tablespoons each of coconut, chocolate chips, crisped rice cereal, and sprinkles on small plates or a plate with sections.

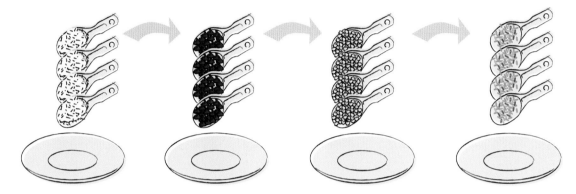

3. Peel the banana. On a cutting board, use a plastic knife to slice it into 4 big pieces. Dip the banana slices in 2 tablespoons of lemon juice and set aside. Using the plastic knife, slice the peach into big slices. You can leave the strawberries whole.

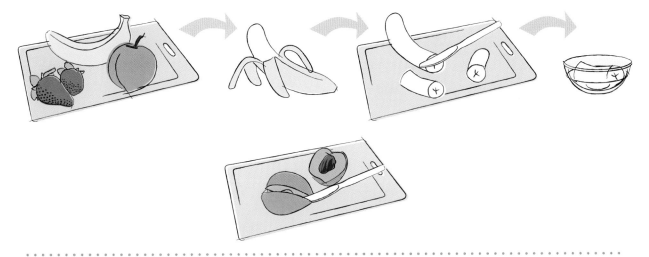

4. Dip each piece of fruit into the peanut butter or spread it on using the butter knife. After each piece is covered in peanut butter, roll it in the various toppings. You can use 1, 2, or all 4!

Honey Mustard Dressing

TOOLS

- **Medium bowl**
- **Measuring cup**
- **Measuring spoons**
- **Wooden spoon**

INGREDIENTS

- **3 tablespoons Dijon mustard**
- **4 tablespoons honey**
- **1 cup mayonnaise**

GROWN-UP PREP: nada

1. Place a bowl securely on your work surface. Plop 3 tablespoons of Dijon mustard, 4 tablespoons of honey, and 1 cup of mayonnaise in the bowl. Using a wooden spoon, stir and stir until everything is mixed together smoothly.

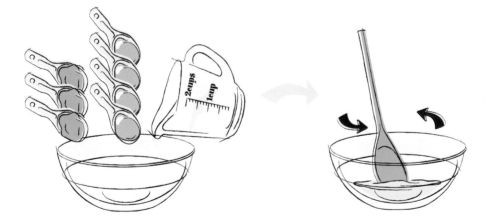

Vinaigrette Dressing

TOOLS

- **Wide-mouth quart jar with tight-fitting lid**
- **Measuring spoons**
- **Measuring cup**

GROWN-UP PREP: none

INGREDIENTS

- 6 tablespoons red wine vinegar
- 2 tablespoons lemon juice
- 2 teaspoons honey
- 1 teaspoon salt
- black pepper
- 1 cup olive oil

1. Place a jar securely on your work surface and unscrew the lid. Add 6 tablespoons of red wine vinegar to the jar. Add 2 tablespoons of lemon juice to the red wine vinegar. Add 2 teaspoons of honey to the jar. Add 1 teaspoon of salt and a few grinds of black pepper.

2. Slowly pour 1 cup of olive oil into the jar. Screw on the lid and close tightly. Hold the jar really tight and shake-shake-shake it for at least 1 minute. If you don't know how long 1 minute is, shake it while you sing "Row, Row, Row Your Boat." That should do it.

Thousand Island Dressing

TOOLS

- Medium bowl
- Measuring cup
- Measuring spoons
- Wooden spoon

GROWN-UP PREP: nothing

INGREDIENTS

- 1 cup mayonnaise
- 5 tablespoons ketchup
- 2 tablespoons pickle relish
- 1/2 teaspoon lemon juice
- 1/2 teaspoon salt

1. Place a bowl securely on your work surface. Plop 1 cup of mayonnaise into the bowl.

2. Add 5 tablespoons of ketchup. Using a wooden spoon, stir until you can't see any white mayonnaise.

3. Add 2 tablespoons of pickle relish, 1/2 teaspoon of lemon juice, and 1/2 teaspoon of salt. Stir well.

TOOLS

- Medium bowl
- Measuring cup
- Measuring spoons
- Wooden spoon
- Cutting board
- Kid scissors

INGREDIENTS

- 1 cup buttermilk
- 6 tablespoons mayonnaise
- 2 teaspoons lemon juice
- 1/8 teaspoon paprika
- 1 teaspoon snipped fresh dill
- 1 tablespoon snipped fresh parsley
- 1/2 teaspoon salt
- 1/4 teaspoon dry mustard

GROWN-UP PREP: nothing

1. Place a bowl securely on your work surface. Add 1 cup of buttermilk and 6 tablespoons of mayonnaise to the bowl. Using a wooden spoon, mix together well.

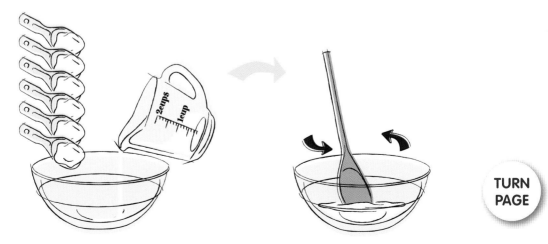

TURN PAGE

2. Add 1/8 teaspoon of paprika and 2 teaspoons of lemon juice and stir some more.

3. Over the cutting board, use the scissors to cut the dill into tiny pieces until you have enough to fill 1 teaspoon. Cut enough parsley to fill 1 tablespoon.

4. Add 1 teaspoon of dill and 1 tablespoon of parsley to the buttermilk mixture and mix. Stir in 1/2 teaspoon of salt and 1/4 teaspoon of dry mustard into the dressing and mix well.

Yogurt Salsa Dressing

TOOLS

- Medium bowl
- Measuring spoons
- Wooden spoon

GROWN-UP PREP: nope

INGREDIENTS

- 1 8-ounce container plain yogurt
- 6 tablespoons mild to medium salsa
- 1 tablespoon ketchup
- 1/4 teaspoon salt

1. Place a bowl securely on your work surface. Empty the yogurt container into the bowl.

2. Add 6 tablespoons of salsa to the bowl. Using a wooden spoon, stir to mix. (If you like your dressing kind of spicy, use a medium salsa.)

3. Add 1 tablespoon of ketchup and 1/4 teaspoon of salt and stir well.

Baby Blue Dressing

TOOLS

- Medium bowl
- Measuring cup
- Wooden spoon
- Measuring spoons

INGREDIENTS

- 1 cup mayonnaise
- 6 tablespoons blue cheese, at room temperature
- 2 tablespoons sour cream
- 1 teaspoon Worcestershire sauce
- 1 teaspoon lemon juice
- 1/2 teaspoon dry mustard
- 1/2 teaspoon garlic powder
- 1/2 teaspoon salt
- black pepper

GROWN-UP PREP: nothing

1. Place a bowl securely on your working surface. Plop 1 cup of mayonnaise into the bowl. Using a wooden spoon, stir until it looks smooth.

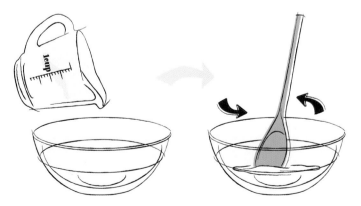

TURN PAGE

2. Add 6 tablespoons of blue cheese and stir again. (Room-temperature blue cheese should mix easily. If it doesn't, use your fingers to crumble the cheese.)

3. Add 2 tablespoons of sour cream and stir until it is well mixed.

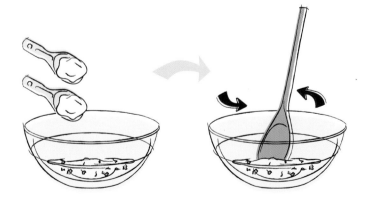

4. Add 1 teaspoon of Worcestershire sauce and 1 teaspoon of lemon juice to the bowl and stir again until smooth.

5. Add 1/2 teaspoon of dry mustard, 1/2 teaspoon of garlic powder, 1/2 teaspoon of salt, and some grinds of black pepper. Stir until it is all mixed together.

Chopped Salad SERVES 4

TOOLS

- **Cutting board**
- **Plastic knife**
- **Salad bowl**
- **Salad spoon and fork**

INGREDIENTS

- 1 head romaine lettuce
- 1 tomato
- 1/2 cucumber
- 4 slices baked ham
- 4 slices roast turkey
- 4 slices Swiss cheese
- 1/2 red pepper
- 6 to 8 tablespoons of your favorite dressing

GROWN-UP PREP: nada

1. On a cutting board, lay out the head of lettuce. Use your hands to pull the lettuce leaves from the head. Then use a plastic knife to chop the leaves into small bite-size pieces. Put the chopped lettuce into the bowl on your work surface.

2. On the cutting board, use the plastic knife to cut the tomato into small bite-sized pieces. Cut the cucumber into thin slices. Then cut each slice into 4 pieces. Try to keep everything small.

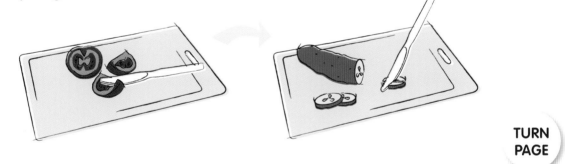

TURN PAGE

3. Cut the ham, turkey, Swiss cheese, and red pepper into small pieces as well.
Put everything into the bowl.

4. Pour 6 to 8 tablespoons of dressing over the salad. Using a salad spoon and fork, mix well.

Fried Chicken Salad SERVES 4

TOOLS

- Cutting board
- Plastic knife
- Fork
- Large bowl
- Measuring cup
- Measuring spoons
- Wooden spoons

INGREDIENTS

- 2 boneless, fried chicken breasts
- 1 head lettuce or small bag mixed greens
- 1 cup cherry tomatoes
- 8 tablespoons shredded Cheddar cheese
- 6 tablespoons baby blue dressing (see page 72)

GROWN-UP PREP: 2 boneless, fried chicken breasts

1. On a cutting board, use a plastic knife and fork to cut the chicken into bite-size pieces. Put the chicken into a bowl on your work surface.

2. Tear the head of lettuce into bite-size pieces and add to the bowl.

3. On the cutting board, use the plastic knife to cut 1 cup of cherry tomatoes in half. Add them to the bowl.

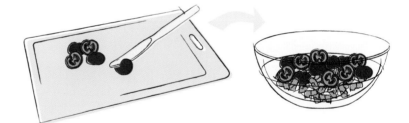

4. Add 8 tablespoons of Cheddar cheese and 6 tablespoons of baby blue dressing to the bowl. Using wooden spoons, mix well and serve.

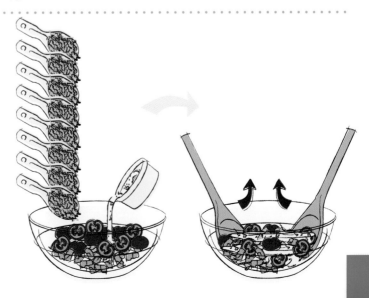

Pasta Salad with Cheese, Tomato, and Pesto SERVES 4

TOOLS

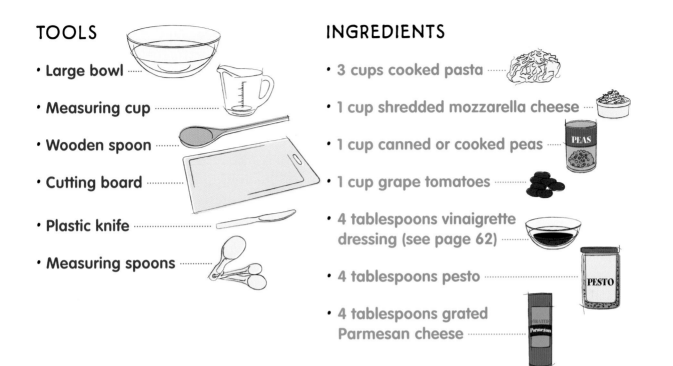

- Large bowl
- Measuring cup
- Wooden spoon
- Cutting board
- Plastic knife
- Measuring spoons

INGREDIENTS

- 3 cups cooked pasta
- 1 cup shredded mozzarella cheese
- 1 cup canned or cooked peas
- 1 cup grape tomatoes
- 4 tablespoons vinaigrette dressing (see page 62)
- 4 tablespoons pesto
- 4 tablespoons grated Parmesan cheese

GROWN-UP PREP: pasta, cooked, drained, and cooled; peas, cooked, drained, and cooled

. . . .

1. Place a large bowl securely on your work surface. Put the cooked pasta into the bowl.

TURN PAGE

2. Add 1 cup of mozzarella cheese and 1 cup of peas. Using a wooden spoon, mix well.

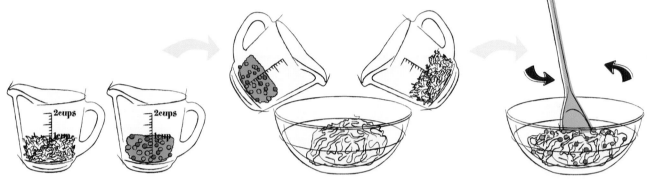

3. On a cutting board, use a plastic knife to cut 1 cup of grape tomatoes in half. Add them to the pasta, cheese, and peas.

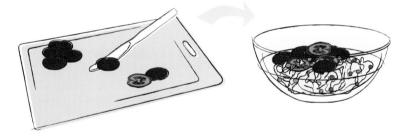

4. Add 4 tablespoons of pesto to the vinaigrette. Use a wooden spoon to mix well.

5. Pour 4 tablespoons of the vinaigrette and pesto dressing over the pasta mixture. Sprinkle with 4 tablespoons of Parmesan cheese and serve.

Rice Salad with Raisins, Berries, and Other Good Stuff SERVES 4

TOOLS

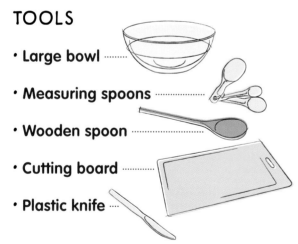

- **Large bowl**
- **Measuring spoons**
- **Wooden spoon**
- **Cutting board**
- **Plastic knife**

INGREDIENTS

- 3 cups cooked jasmine brown rice (or couscous)

- 4 tablespoons golden raisins

- 2 tablespoons dried cranberries

- 2 tablespoons chopped dried apricots

- 8 strawberries

- 8 seedless grapes

- 4 tablespoons vinaigrette dressing (see page 62)

GROWN-UP PREP: rice or couscous, cooked

1. Place a large bowl securely on your work surface. Put the cooked rice (or couscous) into the bowl.

2. Add 4 tablespoons of golden raisins, 2 tablespoons of dried cranberries, and 2 tablespoons of chopped dried apricots to the bowl. Use a wooden spoon to mix.

3. On a cutting board, use a plastic knife to slice the strawberries thinly. Cut the grapes in half. Add the strawberry slices and grape halves to the bowl and mix together with the wooden spoon.

4. Add 4 tablespoons of vinaigrette to the rice or couscous mixture. Using the wooden spoon, stir gently to combine.

87

Sesame Noodle Salad SERVES 4

TOOLS

- **Medium bowl**
- **Measuring spoons**
- **Wooden spoon**
- **Cutting board**
- **Plastic knife**
- **Large bowl**

INGREDIENTS

- 8 tablespoons smooth peanut butter
- 4 tablespoons soy sauce
- 2 tablespoons red wine vinegar
- 1 1/2 tablespoons Asian sesame oil
- 2 teaspoons honey
- 3 pepper halves
- 1 pound cooked linguine or spaghetti noodles

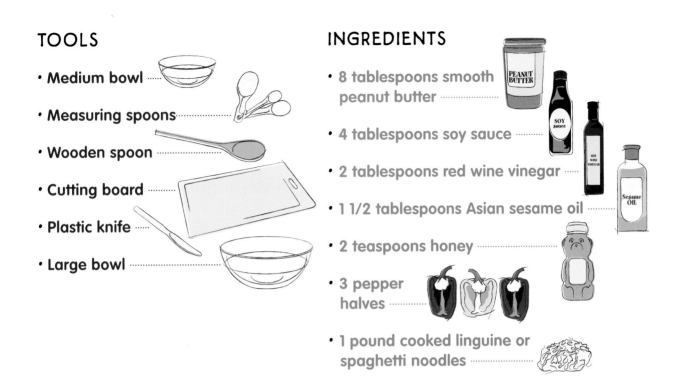

GROWN-UP PREP: noodles, cooked, drained, and cooled

1. Place a medium bowl securely on your work surface. Add 8 tablespoons of peanut butter and 4 tablespoons of soy sauce to the bowl. Using a wooden spoon, stir well.

TURN PAGE

2. Add 5 tablespoons of warm water to the peanut butter mixture and stir again.

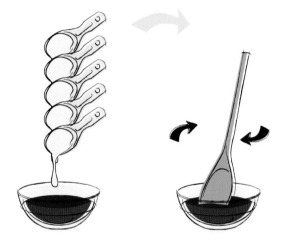

3. Add 2 tablespoons of red wine vinegar, 1 1/2 tablespoons of sesame oil, and 2 teaspoons of honey. Stir to mix everything.

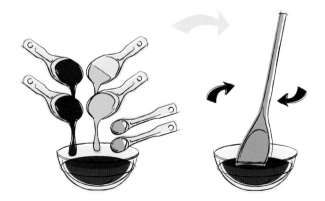

4. On a cutting board, use a plastic knife to cut the peppers into very thin strips.

5. Place the noodles and the cut-up peppers into a large bowl. Add the peanut sauce and mix everything together well.

Triple Bean Salad SERVES 4

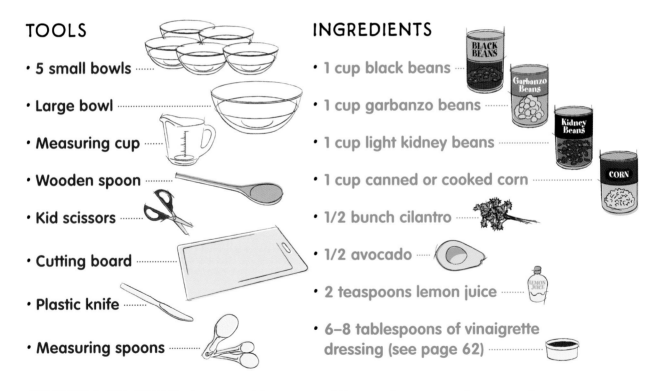

TOOLS

- 5 small bowls
- Large bowl
- Measuring cup
- Wooden spoon
- Kid scissors
- Cutting board
- Plastic knife
- Measuring spoons

INGREDIENTS

- 1 cup black beans
- 1 cup garbanzo beans
- 1 cup light kidney beans
- 1 cup canned or cooked corn
- 1/2 bunch cilantro
- 1/2 avocado
- 2 teaspoons lemon juice
- 6–8 tablespoons of vinaigrette dressing (see page 62)

GROWN-UP PREP: 3 types of beans and 1 can of corn, each opened and drained into separate bowls; 1 avocado, pitted and peeled

1. Place a large bowl on your work surface. Put 1 cup each of the black beans, garbanzo beans, and kidney beans into the large bowl. Add 1 cup of corn. Using a wooden spoon, stir to mix.

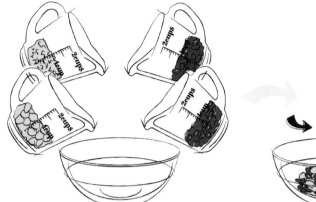

2. Over the bowl, use scissors to snip the cilantro into very small pieces.

3. On a cutting board, use a plastic knife to cut the avocado into small chunks. Place the avocado into a small bowl. Add 2 teaspoons of lemon juice and mix well. (The lemon juice will keep the avocado from turning brown.)

4. Add the avocado to the bean mixture. Add 6 to 8 tablespoons of vinaigrette dressing and mix well.

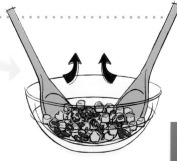

Corn Salad SERVES 4

TOOLS

- **Cutting board**
- **Plastic knife**
- **Large bowl**
- **Wooden spoon**
- **Measuring spoons**

INGREDIENTS

- 1/2 orange pepper
- 1/2 red pepper
- 1 ripe tomato
- 1 16-ounce package frozen corn
- 5 tablespoons yogurt salsa dressing (see page 70)

GROWN-UP PREP: frozen corn, thawed and drained

1. On a cutting board, use a plastic knife to cut the peppers into small pieces. Put the pepper pieces into a bowl placed securely on your work surface.

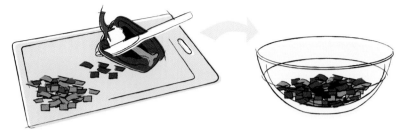

2. On the cutting board, use the plastic knife to cut the tomato into small pieces. Add tomato to the bowl.

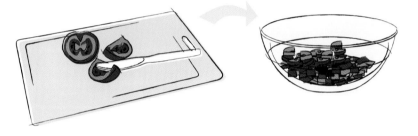

3. Put the corn into the bowl. Using a wooden spoon, mix ingredients together. Add 5 tablespoons of dressing and stir until well mixed.

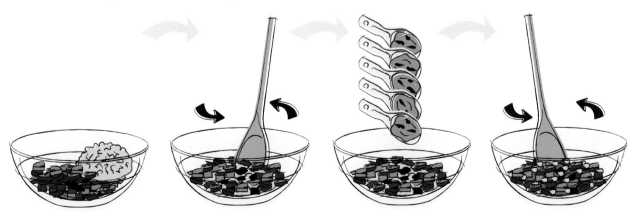

SALADS, DRESSINGS, & DIPS

Potato Salad SERVES 4

TOOLS

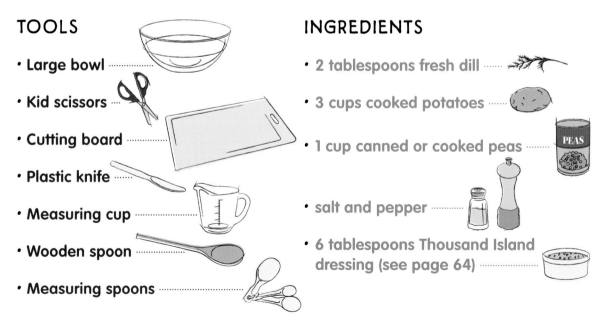

- Large bowl
- Kid scissors
- Cutting board
- Plastic knife
- Measuring cup
- Wooden spoon
- Measuring spoons

INGREDIENTS

- 2 tablespoons fresh dill
- 3 cups cooked potatoes
- 1 cup canned or cooked peas
- salt and pepper
- 6 tablespoons Thousand Island dressing (see page 64)

GROWN-UP PREP: potatoes and peas, cooked, drained, and cooled

96

1. Place a bowl securely on your work surface. Over the bowl, use scissors to finely cut up about 2 tablespoons of dill.

2. On a cutting board, use a plastic knife to cut the potatoes into bite-size chunks. Add to the bowl.

3. Add 1 cup of peas to bowl. Add a pinch of salt and a few grinds of pepper. Using a wooden spoon, gently stir ingredients together.

4. Add 6 tablespoons of Thousand Island dressing to the bowl. Using a wooden spoon, stir ingredients and you're done.

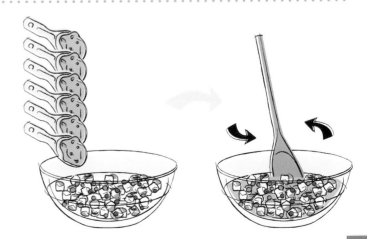

Frozen Honey-Dipped Bananas

TOOLS

- Wax paper
- Baking sheet
- Cutting board
- Plastic knife
- Measuring spoons
- 4 wooden pop sticks
- 3 small plates
- Measuring cup

GROWN-UP PREP: nada

INGREDIENTS

- 2 bananas
- 3 tablespoons lemon juice
- 2 tablespoons honey
- 1 cup crisped rice cereal

- 1 cup colored sprinkles

1. Place a sheet of wax paper on a baking sheet.

2. Peel the bananas. On a cutting board, use a plastic knife to cut them in half crosswise. Put 3 tablespoons of lemon juice on the wax paper sheet and roll the banana pieces in the lemon juice. Stick a wooden pop stick into the bottom of each banana piece. Slide them in the freezer until frozen.

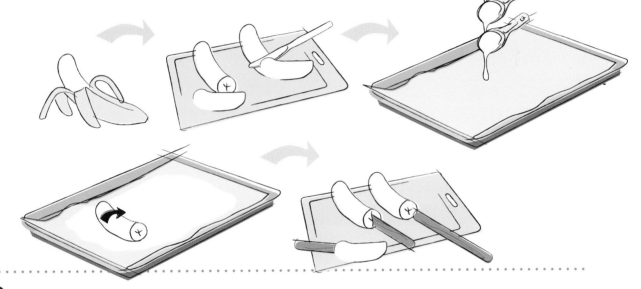

3. When you're ready to eat the banana pops, squeeze some honey onto a plate. Pour 1 cup of sprinkles on another plate and 1 cup of cereal on a third plate. Twirl a banana piece in the honey, covering it as much as you can. Then, roll the banana in sprinkles, cereal, or both. Repeat with each banana pop.

Fresh Fruit and Yogurt Cones

TOOLS

- Cutting board
- Plastic knife
- Measuring spoons

INGREDIENTS

- 2 strawberries
- 1 flat-bottom ice cream cone
- 6 raspberries
- 6 blueberries
- 2 tablespoons flavored yogurt

GROWN-UP PREP: nada

1. On a cutting board, use a plastic knife to thinly slice the strawberries.

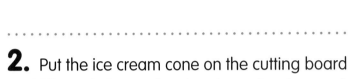

2. Put the ice cream cone on the cutting board and fill it with 2 strawberries, 6 raspberries, and 6 blueberries.

3. Drizzle 2 tablespoons of yogurt on top of the fruit.

Ice Cream Cookie Sandwich with Sprinkles SERVES 4

TOOLS

- Cutting board
- Ice cream scoop
- Measuring spoons
- Small plate

GROWN-UP PREP: nothing

INGREDIENTS

- 1 pint ice cream, any flavor
- 8 pretty big cookies, any flavor
- 8 tablespoons chocolate or colored sprinkles

1. Take the ice cream out of the freezer and let it sit to soften about 10 minutes. Use a timer or sing 3 or 4 different songs while you wait.

2. Place 4 cookies on your cutting board. As soon as the ice cream is soft enough, scoop out 4 portions and place one on each cookie.

3. Place 4 remaining cookies on top of ice cream.

4. Put 8 tablespoons of sprinkles on a plate. Roll the edges of the cookies in the sprinkles. Place the cookies back in the freezer until they freeze again, about 20 minutes.

DESSERTS

Indoors S'mores

TOOLS

- Cutting board
- Measuring spoons
- Butter knife

GROWN-UP PREP: nothing

INGREDIENTS

- 4 double graham crackers
- 4 tablespoons chocolate frosting
- 4 tablespoons marshmallow creme

1. Over a cutting board, break 4 double graham crackers in half along the scored line. Now you have 8 square crackers.

2. Using a butter knife, spread 1 tablespoon of the frosting onto each of the 4 graham cracker squares.

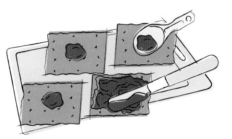

3. Using a butter knife, spread 1 tablespoon of the marshmallow creme onto each of the 4 remaining graham crackers.

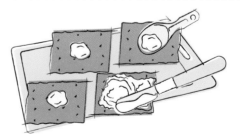

4. Put the crackers together so the chocolate frosting is pressed up against the marshmallow creme.

Strawberry Tall Cake

TOOLS

- Cutting board
- Plastic knife
- Medium bowl
- Rectangular platter
- Measuring spoons

INGREDIENTS

- 12 large strawberries
- 1 frozen pound cake, defrosted
- 10 tablespoons strawberry syrup
- 1 can whipped cream

GROWN-UP PREP: pound cake, defrosted and sliced horizontally into 3 equal pieces

1. On a cutting board, use a plastic knife to thinly slice the strawberries. (Save 1 whole strawberry.) Place a bowl securely on your work surface and put the strawberries in it.

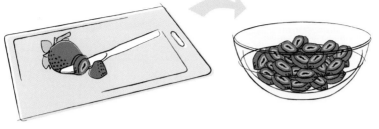

2. Place the platter on your work surface. Put the bottom slice of cake on the platter. Spread about half of the strawberries over the cake slice. Drizzle the strawberries with 5 tablespoons of strawberry syrup. Cover the berries with whipped cream. (Shake well and squirt! But not too close to the berries!)

TURN PAGE

3. Place another slice of cake on top of the whipped cream. Place almost half the remaining strawberries on the cake slice and again drizzle with 5 tablespoons of strawberry syrup. Again, cover the berries in whipped cream.

4. Place the last slice of the pound cake on the layered cake. Top with the remaining berry slices and 1 whole berry.

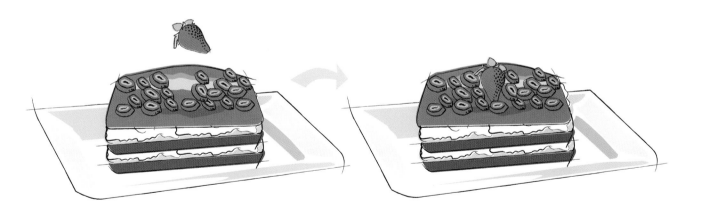

Tiny Trifle

TOOLS

- Ziploc® bag
- 4 custard cups
- Measuring spoons
- Medium bowl
- Measuring cup
- Hand mixer

GROWN-UP PREP: none

INGREDIENTS

- 16 vanilla wafers
- 32 raspberries
- 8 tablespoons chocolate syrup
- 1 small package instant vanilla pudding mix
- 2 cups 2% milk

1. Put 16 vanilla wafers into the Ziploc® bag and close it securely. Press down on the cookies in the bag to crush them into chunks. DO NOT turn them into crumbs—there should be some big pieces.

2. Place 4 custard cups securely on your work surface. Put 2 tablespoons of the cookie crumbles in the bottom of each cup.

TURN PAGE

3. Place 4 raspberries on each pile of crumbles. Drizzle 1 tablespoon of chocolate syrup on each cup of berries.

4. Make the instant pudding by mixing the milk with the pudding powder and using the mixer to beat until the pudding is completely smooth. Plop equal amounts of pudding into each of the 4 custard cups.

5. Put the cups in the refrigerator for about 10 minutes. Use a timer or sing 3 or 4 different songs while you wait. Take the cups out of the fridge.

6. Add 4 raspberries to each cup. Sprinkle each cup with some of the cookie pieces and top each cup with 1 tablespoon of chocolate syrup.

Egg Cream

TOOLS

- Tall drinking glass
- Measuring cup
- Measuring spoons
- Wooden spoon

GROWN-UP PREP: nothing

INGREDIENTS

- 1/2 cup cold milk
- 1 cup cold seltzer
- 2 tablespoons chocolate syrup

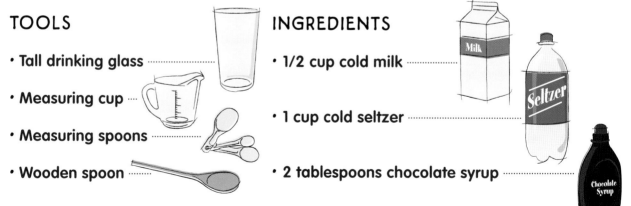

1. Place a tall glass securely on your work surface.
Pour in 1/2 cup of milk.

2. Pour 1 cup of seltzer into the glass.

3. Add 2 tablespoons of chocolate syrup and stir with a wooden spoon to mix.
NOTE: Drink within 5 minutes or the fizz (and the thrill) will be gone.

Orange Juice Strawberry Spritzer

TOOLS

- Tall drinking glass
- Measuring cup
- Cutting board
- Plastic knife
- Measuring spoons
- Wooden spoon

INGREDIENTS

- 1 cup orange juice
- 2 strawberries
- 4 tablespoons Sprite® or seltzer

GROWN-UP PREP: nada

1. Place a tall glass securely on your work surface. Add 1 cup of orange juice. Set the glass aside.

2. On a cutting board, use a plastic knife to cut the strawberries into thin slices.

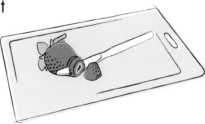

3. Add the berries to the juice. Just before drinking, add 4 tablespoons of Sprite® or seltzer. Stir and enjoy.

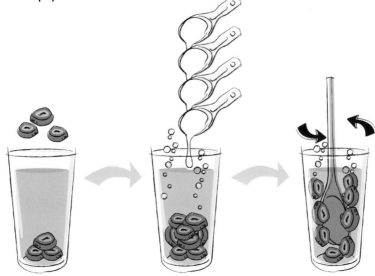

DRINKS | # Fruity Ice Cubes

TOOLS

- Measuring cup with spout ......
- Ice cube tray ......

INGREDIENTS

- 1 cup water ......
- 24 raspberries ......
- 12 mint leaves ......

GROWN-UP PREP: nada

1. Using the measuring cup with a spout, fill each section of an ice cube tray half full with water.

2. Put 2 raspberries and 1 mint leaf in each section. Place the ice cube tray in the freezer for 30 minutes. Use a timer or watch an episode of one of your favorite cartoons.

3. Remove the tray from the freezer. Fill the sections, covering the fruit with water. Freeze again until solid. Drop ice cubes into water, seltzer, or lemonade for a pretty, refreshing drink.

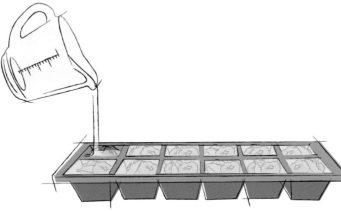

Kid Sangria

TOOLS

- Large plastic pitcher
- Measuring cups
- Cutting board
- Plastic knife
- Wooden spoon

INGREDIENTS

- 3 cups orange juice
- 1 cup pink lemonade
- 1 cup white grape juice
- 1 cup pineapple juice
- 12 strawberries
- 24 raspberries
- 1 peach

GROWN-UP PREP: nope

1. Place a large plastic pitcher securely on your work surface.
Pour 3 cups of orange juice, 1 cup of pink lemonade,
1 cup of white grape juice, and 1 cup of pineapple juice
into the pitcher. Set aside.

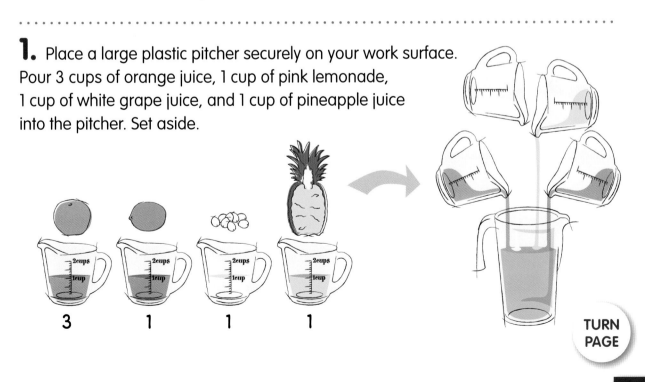

3   1   1   1

TURN PAGE

2. On a cutting board, use a plastic knife to cut the strawberries into thin slices. Put them in the pitcher. Add the 24 raspberries to the pitcher.

1. Place a large plastic pitcher securely on your work surface.
Pour 3 cups of orange juice, 1 cup of pink lemonade,
1 cup of white grape juice, and 1 cup of pineapple juice
into the pitcher. Set aside.

Raspberry Lemonade

TOOLS

- Large plastic pitcher
- Measuring cup
- Wooden spoon
- Medium bowl

INGREDIENTS

- 1 cup lemon juice
- 1 cup super fine sugar
- 4 cups water
- 20 fresh raspberries

GROWN-UP PREP: nothing

1. Place a large plastic pitcher securely on your work surface. Add 1 cup of super fine sugar and 1 cup of lemon juice to the pitcher. Using a wooden spoon, stir to dissolve the sugar.

TURN PAGE

2. Add 4 cups of water to the pitcher and stir again.

3. Place a medium bowl securely on your work surface. Put the raspberries into the bowl and mash them with the wooden spoon. (No need to completely squish, just mash a little to get them really juicy.)

4. Add the raspberries to the pitcher and stir with the wooden spoon one last time.

MOSTLY MAIN INGREDIENT INDEX

If you've got left-over rice, are drowning in crackers, or have a craving for bananas, this will steer you to the right recipe.